info buzz

Queen Victoria

Izzi Howell

W
FRANKLIN WATTS
LONDON•SYDNEY

Franklin Watts
First published in Great Britain in 2018 by The Watts Publishing Group
Copyright © The Watts Publishing Group, 2018

 Produced for Franklin Watts by
White-Thomson Publishing Ltd
www.wtpub.co.uk

Credits
Series Editor: Izzi Howell
Series Designer: Rocket Design (East Anglia) Ltd
Designer: Clare Nicholas
Literacy Consultant: Kate Ruttle

The publisher would like to thank the following for permission to reproduce their pictures: Alamy: Peter Horree 4, Historical Images Archive 6t, Chronicle 7t, Lebrecht Music and Arts Photo Library 10, Heritage Image Partnership Ltd 14, Pictorial Press Ltd 15, INTERFOTO 19l; Getty: Heritage Images 11, Hulton Archive 18, Hulton Archive 19r; Shutterstock: Everett – Art title page and 8, Everett Historical 5 and 9, Aivita Arika 6–7b, Cat Act Art 13t, Olesya Tseytlin 13c, Lotus Images 13bl, Ines Behrens-Kunkel 13br, jgorzynik 16, LiliGraphie 17t, Paul Michael Hughes 17bl, Leigh Prather 17br, Featureflash Photo Agency 20, Przemyslaw Skibinski 21l, Gary Blakeley 21r; Stefan Chabluk 12; Superstock: Stock Montage cover.

Every attempt has been made to clear copyright. Should there be any inadvertent omission please apply to the publisher for rectification.

Printed in China

Franklin Watts
An imprint of
Hachette Children's Group
Part of The Watts Publishing Group
Carmelite House
50 Victoria Embankment
London EC4Y 0DZ

An Hachette UK Company
www.hachette.co.uk
www.franklinwatts.co.uk

All words in **bold** appear in the glossary on page 23.

Contents

Who was Queen Victoria?

Victoria was the Queen of the **United Kingdom** (UK) from 1837 to 1901. She also **ruled** over other countries including Australia and New Zealand.

◀ Victoria often wore a crown and expensive clothes.

What differences can you see between the pictures of Queen Victoria here and on page 4?

Victoria was Queen for 63 years. This is longer than any other British king or queen, except for Queen Elizabeth II (Second).

▲ Victoria ruled until she was 81 years old.

5

Childhood

Princess Victoria was born on 24 May 1819. Her father died when she was a baby. She lived with her mother.

◀ This painting shows Victoria when she was four years old.

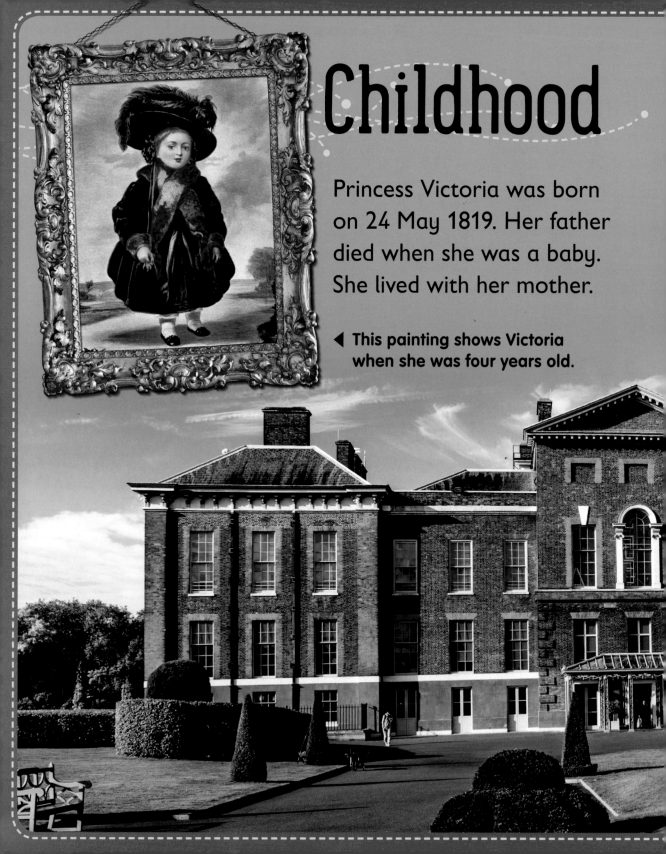

Victoria did not go to school. A teacher taught her on her own at home. She liked to draw and play with dolls and her pets.

Victoria loved ▶ her pet dogs.

Victoria and her mother lived in Kensington Palace in London. ▼

Becoming Queen

In 1837, Victoria's uncle King William IV (Fourth) died. William didn't have any children, so Victoria became Queen.

◀ Victoria was 18 years old when she became Queen.

How do you think Victoria felt when she became Queen?

In 1938, Victoria **celebrated** her **coronation**. 400,000 people came to London for the coronation.

▲ Victoria's coronation was in Westminster Abbey – a large church in London.

Marriage and children

In 1840, Victoria married Prince Albert. Albert was from Germany.

▼ Victoria wore a white dress on her wedding day.

What kinds of clothes are Victoria's children wearing? What do children wear today?

Victoria and Albert had nine children — five girls and four boys.

▲
Victoria and Albert with five of their children.

Around the world

Victoria was Queen of the **British Empire**. She ruled over countries in the British Empire, such as Australia, India, South Africa and Canada.

Canada

United Kingdom

India

Egypt

Gambia

Sudan

British Guiana

Sierra Leone

Gold Coast

Kenya

Nigeria

Singapore

South Africa

Australia

New Zealand

▲ The pink areas show the British Empire when Victoria was Queen.

Countries in the British Empire **traded** with each other. The UK made a lot of money from trade.

Countries in the British Empire traded tea, coffee and cotton.
▼

coffee beans

cotton plant

cotton cloth

tea

What do you think cotton plants feel like?

13

Sad times

In 1861, Prince Albert became very ill. The doctors didn't know how to make him better. He died in December 1861.

◀ Albert was only 42 years old when he died.

Queen Victoria was very sad after Albert's death. She didn't go out **in public** often. She spent most of her time with her family.

▼ Queen Victoria only wore black clothes for the rest of her life. This showed people that she was still sad.

Change

We use the word 'Victorian' to describe the years in which Victoria was Queen. There were many changes in the British Empire during Victorian times.

People built railway lines across the UK in Victorian times.
▼

How do you think people travelled around before railways were built?

Many people moved to cities from the countryside. They worked in new **factories**.

There were new inventions in Victorian times.
▼

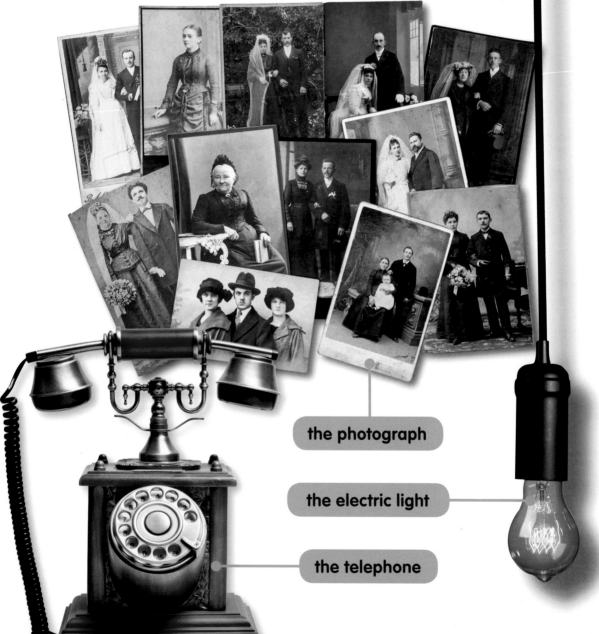

the photograph

the electric light

the telephone

Later years

Queen Victoria ruled for many years. In 1887, she celebrated her Golden **Jubilee** after ruling for 50 years.

▼ In 1897, Victoria rode through London in a carriage to celebrate her Diamond Jubilee – 60 years of being Queen.

Queen Victoria died on 22 January 1901.
She was 81 years old.

◀ Victoria was buried
in the same place
as Albert, near
Windsor Castle.

▼ Victoria's oldest
son became
King Edward VII
(Seventh).

Remembering Victoria

Today, many kings and queens in Europe are **descendants** of Victoria.

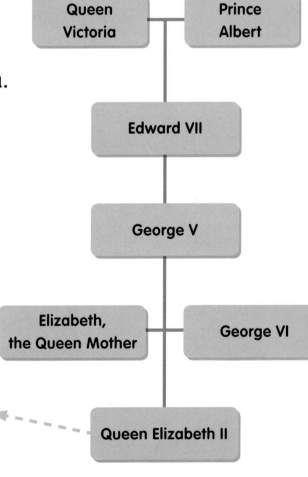

Queen Victoria	Prince Albert

Edward VII

George V

Elizabeth, the Queen Mother	George VI

Queen Elizabeth II

▲ Queen Elizabeth II is Queen Victoria's great-great-granddaughter.

There are many places named after Queen Victoria. The state of Victoria in Australia and Lake Victoria in Africa are both named after her.

▲ The Victoria Cross is a medal given to brave people.

▲ Victoria Falls is an African waterfall named after Queen Victoria.

Do you know anything else named after Queen Victoria?

21

Quiz

Test how much you remember.

Check your answers on page 24.

1 For how many years did Victoria rule?

2 How old was Victoria when she became Queen?

3 How many children did Victoria have?

4 Was Australia in the British Empire?

5 What did Victoria celebrate at her Diamond Jubilee?

6 Who was King after Victoria?

Glossary

British Empire – a group of countries ruled by the UK in the past

bury – to put a dead body into the ground

carriage – a vehicle with wheels that is pulled by a horse

celebrate – to do something fun on a special day

coronation – a ceremony at which someone is made the king or the queen

descendant – a child or grandchild who lives after you

factory – a building where machines make products

in public – where lots of people are

invention – something that has never been made before

jubilee – a celebration of an important event in the past

rule – to be in control of a country

trade – to buy and sell products between different countries

United Kingdom – a country that includes England, Scotland, Wales and Northern Ireland

Index

Answers:

1: 63 years; 2: 18 years old; 3: Nine; 4: Yes; 5: 60 years of being Queen;
6: King Edward VII (Seventh)

Teaching notes:

Children who are reading Book band Purple or above should be able to enjoy this book with some independence. Other children will need more support.

Before you share the book:

- What do the children already know about Queen Victoria? Have they heard the word Victorian? Talk about the context (e.g. building, invention)
- When do children think Queen Victoria lived?

While you share the book:

- Help children to read some of the more unfamiliar words.
- Talk about the questions.

- Discuss information about Queen Victoria's life. What might be the same today? What might be different?
- Talk about the pictures. Encourage children to talk about the clothes people are wearing.

After you have shared the book:

- Help children to find out more about the inventions of the Victorian times. Discuss how the inventions have changed since Victorian times.
- If there are Victorian buildings near the school, take children to look at them and talk about what life was like for people who lived in them.
- Work through free activity sheets at www.hachetteschools.co.uk

History

Neil Armstrong

978 1 4451 5948 5

Who was
Neil Armstrong?
Growing up
The Space Race
Neil and NASA
Space training
Lift off!
Walking on the Moon
Back to Earth
Later years

Queen Elizabeth II

978 1 4451 5886 0

Who is
Queen Elizabeth II?
What does the
Queen do?
Around the world
Childhood
Marriage and children
Becoming Queen
The royal family
Special days
At home

Queen Victoria

978 1 4451 5950 8

Who was
Queen Victoria?
Childhood
Becoming Queen
Marriage and children
Around the world
Sad times
Change
Later years
Remembering Victoria

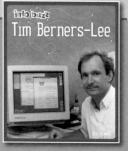

Tim Berners-Lee

978 1 4451 5952 2

Who is
Tim Berners-Lee?
Childhood
University
A new job
Back to CERN
The World Wide Web
Across the world
The Web today
After the Web

Religion

Christianity

978 1 4451 5962 1

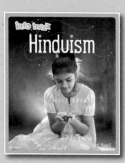

Hinduism

978 1 4451 5964 5

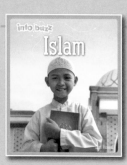

Islam

978 1 4451 5968 3

Judaism

978 1 4451 5966 9

Countries

Argentina

978 1 4451 5958 4

India

978 1 4451 5960 7

Japan

978 1 4451 5956 0

The United Kingdom

978 1 4451 5954 6

FRANKLIN
WATTS